A R

PAUL THE PITCHER

Written and Illustrated
By Paul Sharp

Prepared under the direction of Robert Hillerich, Ph.D.

CHILDRENS PRESS™
CHICAGO

This book is for Seth

Library of Congress Cataloging in Publication Data

Sharp, Paul.
Paul the pitcher.

(A Rookie reader)
Summary: Rhymed text describes the different things Paul enjoys when he throws a ball. Includes word list.
[1. Baseball—Fiction. 2. Stories in rhyme]
I. Title. II. Series.
PZ8.3.S532Pau 1984 [E] 84-7071
ISBN 0-516-02064-1

Printed in the United States of America
3 4 5 6 7 8 9 10 R 93 92 91 90 89 88 87 86 85

Paul the pitcher throws a ball.

Baseball is the game for Paul.

Paul the pitcher throws a ball.

He throws the ball
from spring till fall.

He throws it to the catcher's mitt,

unless the batter gets a hit.

Paul the pitcher loves to throw,

sometimes high,

sometimes low.

Paul the pitcher loves to throw,

sometimes fast,

sometimes slow.

To throw the ball is lots of fun,

unless the batter gets a run.

Paul the pitcher loves to throw.

Someday he'd like to be a pro.

WORD LIST

a
ball
baseball
batter
be
catcher's
fall
fast
for
from
fun
game
gets
he
he'd
high
hit
is
it
like
lots
loves
low
mitt
of
Paul
pitcher
pro
run
slow
someday
sometimes
spring
the
throw(s)
till
to
unless

About the Author/Illustrator

Paul Sharp graduated from the Art Institute of Pittsburgh with a degree in Visual Communications.

He has done illustrations for numerous children's books and magazines. This is the fifth book Paul has illustrated for Childrens Press. He also wrote it.

Paul presently lives, and works as an artist, in Lafayette, Indiana.

Date Due

Se 23 92			

BRODART, INC. Cat. No. 23 233 Printed in U.S.A.